Joy! Joy! Joy!
The Anthem for Black Girls

By Nzinga-Christina Reid, LMSW
Illustrated by Howard Barry

Dedicated to
Nubia Trinity Reid
My Joy

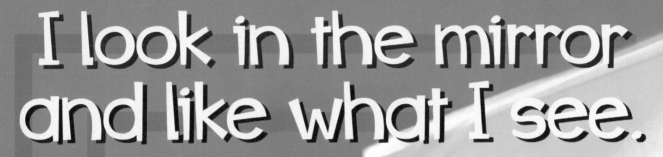

I look in the mirror and like what I see.

From my kinky hair
to my nose, lips, and eyes.

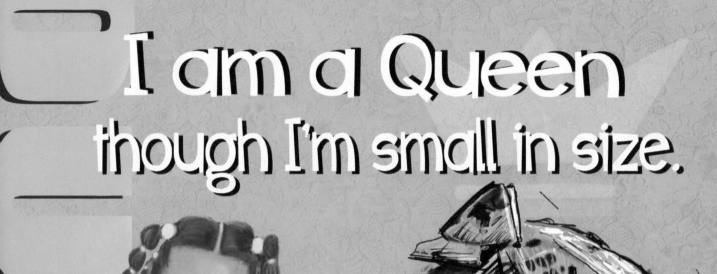

I am a Queen
though I'm small in size.

Joy, joy, joy
all over me!

This Black girl's joy means I LOVE ME

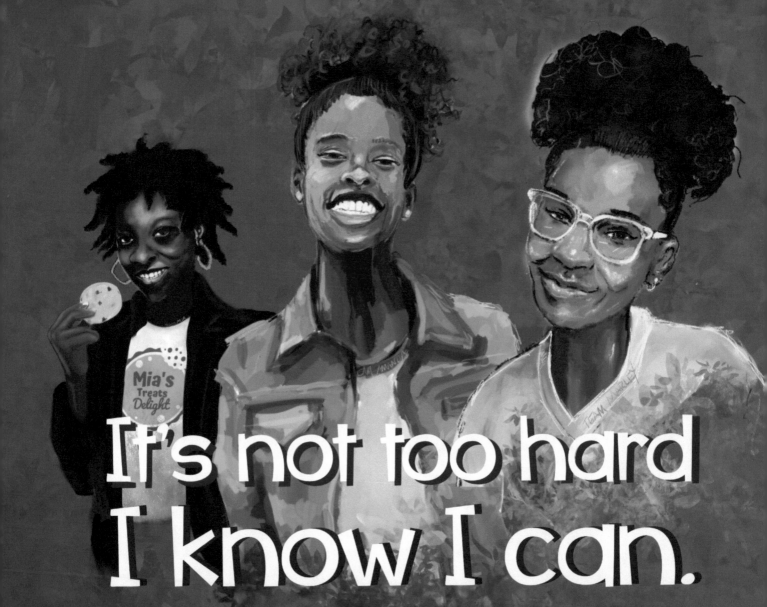

It's not too hard
I know I can.

Science,
Tech,
Engineering,
and Math
too.

Joy, Joy, Joy
all over me

This Black girl's Joy
the World will see!

I'll give respect to
the Misses and Misters.

Let's not forget the brothers, too

I'll show them Love for all they do.

Joy, Joy, Joy
All over me

This Black girl's Joy means Unity

I may fall down when times get tough

But I am strong
I'll get back
Up!

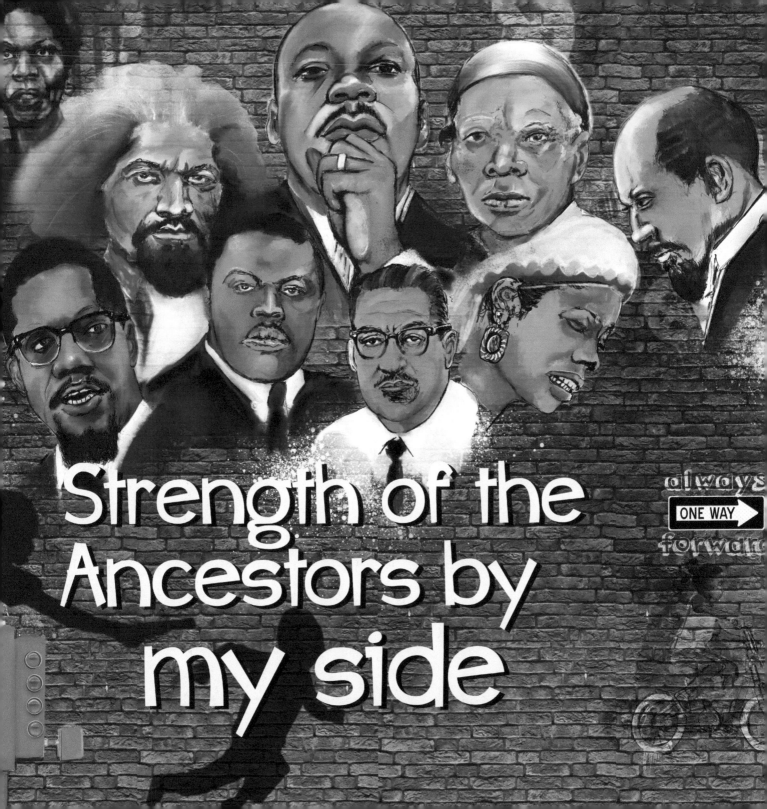

Strength of the Ancestors by my side

always ONE WAY → forward

Joy, Joy, Joy
All over me

This Black girl's joy
means let me be!

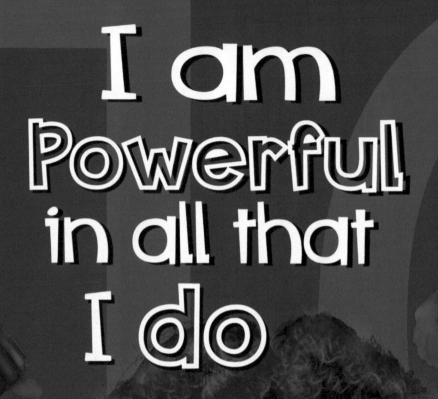

I am
Powerful
in all that
I do

I'll speak my **Goals** and **watch** them come **true.**

And when in doubt
or even Afraid

I'll think of
this Anthem
and here's what
I'll say

Joy, Joy, Joy
All over
Me

This Black girl's Joy
means I Love me

This Black girl's Joy
the World will see

This Black girl's Joy
means I am
Free

CPSIA information can be obtained
at www.ICGtesting.com
Printed in the USA
BVHW021914171021
619163BV00011B/49